Date: 1/25/22

**J 994 LON
London, Martha,
Uluru /**

ENGINEERED BY NATURE

ULURU

BY MARTHA LONDON

CONTENT CONSULTANT
TIMOTHY ROWSE
EMERITUS PROFESSOR
INSTITUTE FOR CULTURE AND SOCIETY
WESTERN SYDNEY UNIVERSITY

Kids Core
An Imprint of Abdo Publishing
abdobooks.com

abdobooks.com

Published by Abdo Publishing, a division of ABDO, PO Box 398166, Minneapolis, Minnesota 55439. Copyright © 2021 by Abdo Consulting Group, Inc. International copyrights reserved in all countries. No part of this book may be reproduced in any form without written permission from the publisher. Kids Core™ is a trademark and logo of Abdo Publishing.

Printed in the United States of America, North Mankato, Minnesota
042020
092020

THIS BOOK CONTAINS RECYCLED MATERIALS

Cover Photo: BM Photographer/Shutterstock Images
Interior Photos: Maurizio De Mattei/Shutterstock Images, 4–5, 25; Shutterstock Images, 7 (Uluru), 7 (Eiffel Tower), 7 (Empire State Building); Benny Marty/Shutterstock Images, 8, 19, 20, 22–23; Tom Jastram/Shutterstock Images, 10–11; DigitalGlobe/Getty Images, 12; John Gaffen/Alamy, 14; Mark Kolbe/Getty Images News/Getty Images, 16–17; Giuglio Gil/Hemis/Alamy, 26; Filed Image/Shutterstock Images, 28; Red Line Editorial, 28–29

Editor: Marie Pearson
Series Designer: Megan Ellis

Library of Congress Control Number: 2019954247

Publisher's Cataloging-in-Publication Data

Names: London, Martha, author.
Title: Uluru / by Martha London
Description: Minneapolis, Minnesota : Abdo Publishing, 2021 | Series: Engineered by nature | Includes online resources and index.
Identifiers: ISBN 9781532192906 (lib. bdg.) | ISBN 9781098210809 (ebook)
Subjects: LCSH: Uluru-Kata Tjuta National Park (N.T.)--Juvenile literature. | Natural monuments--Juvenile literature. | Scenic landscapes--Juvenile literature. | National parks and reserves--Juvenile literature. | Landforms--Juvenile literature.
Classification: DDC 910.202--dc23

CONTENTS

CHAPTER 1
Uluru Sunset 4

CHAPTER 2
From Sea to Desert 10

CHAPTER 3
Caves and Waterfalls 16

CHAPTER 4
In the Future 22

Map 28
Glossary 30
Online Resources 31
Learn More 31
Index 32
About the Author 32

Uluru is especially beautiful at sunset.

CHAPTER **1**

ULURU SUNSET

The sun sinks lower in the sky. The sky bursts with color. Uluru turns from brown to orange and red. The giant, rough rock looks as if it is glowing. A guide takes tourists on the path around it. Sunrise and sunset are the best times to see Uluru.

The hike winds around Uluru. There are cliffs. Waterfalls form after a rainfall. The guide talks about some of the caves. Uluru is a beautiful landform. It is a monolith. A monolith is a large rock formation that rises out of the ground. It took millions of years to form. It is one of the largest monoliths in the world. Uluru is 1,142 feet (348 m) tall. It is 5.8 miles (9.4 km) around. Uluru is made of **sandstone**. This stone gives Uluru its red color.

Do Not Climb

Uluru was closed to climbers in 2019. Climbing Uluru is disrespectful to Anangu people, who own the land. People can still hike around it.

How Tall Is Uluru?

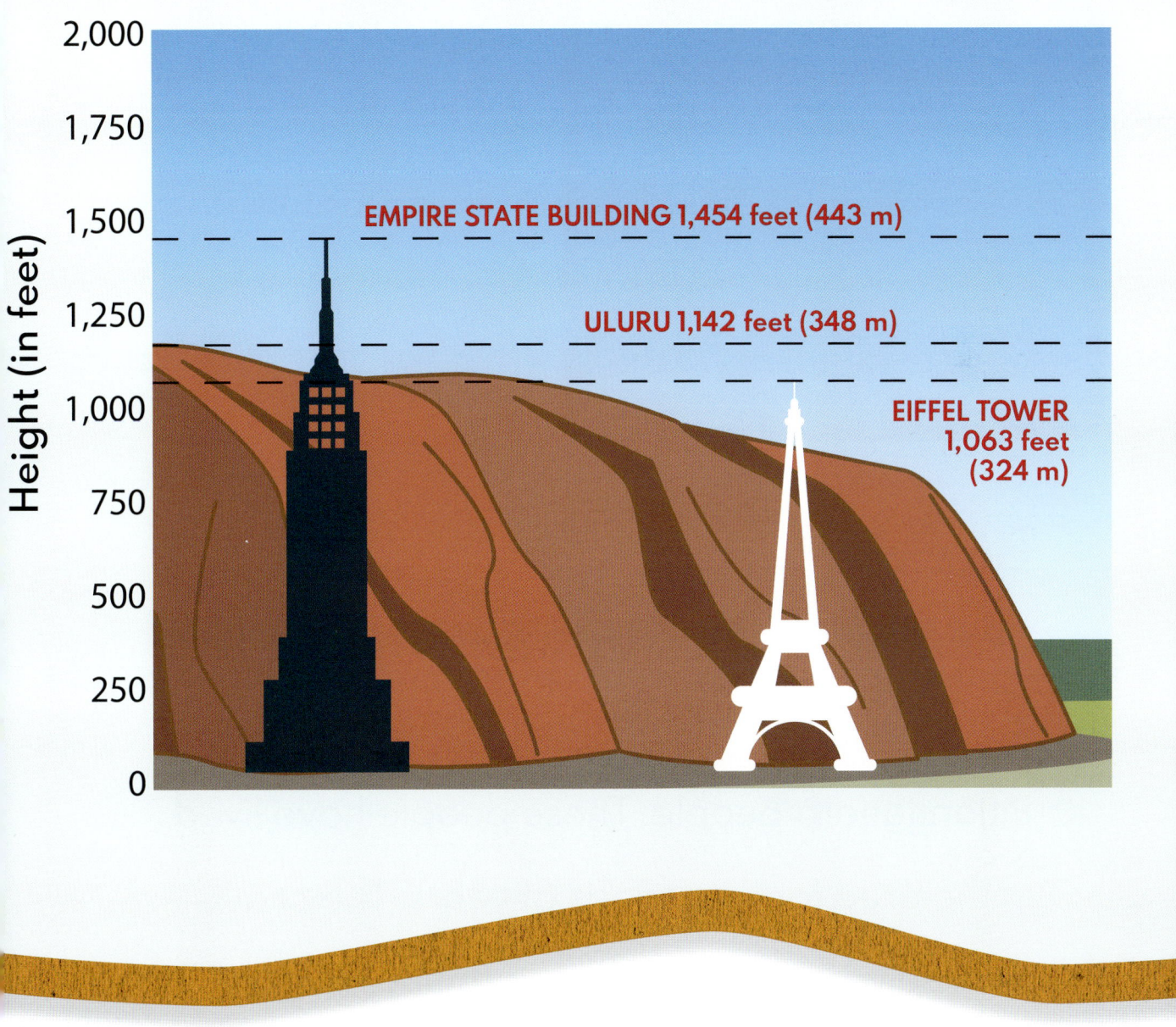

Uluru is a very tall rock formation. At its highest point, it is taller than the Eiffel Tower!

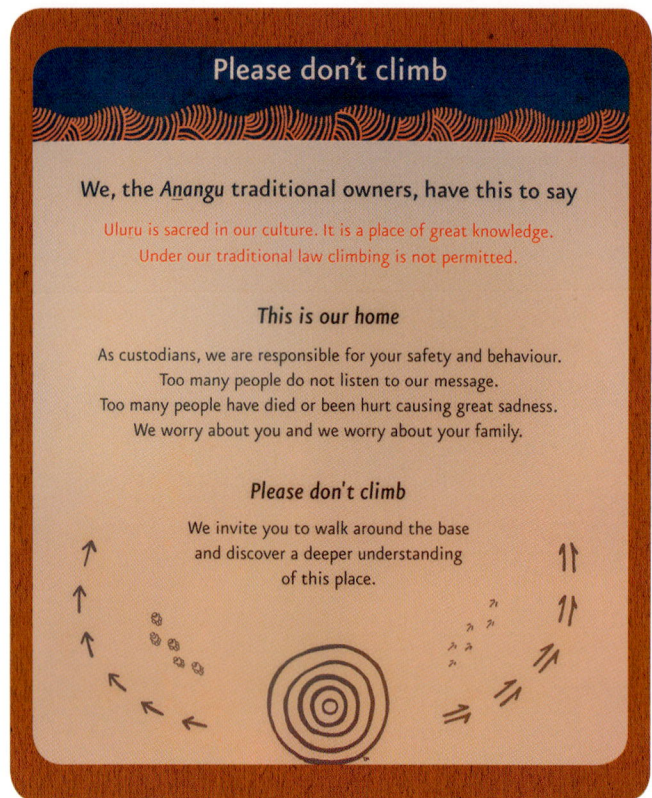

It is important that visitors respect Anangu. This includes not taking pictures of Anangu without permission.

Beautiful Rock

Uluru is an important landform to all people in Australia. Uluru is on the land of the Pitjantjatjara people. These people have lived in the area for thousands of years. They call themselves *Anangu*, which is their word for "people." Uluru is **sacred** to them. Wind and rain continue to shape Uluru.

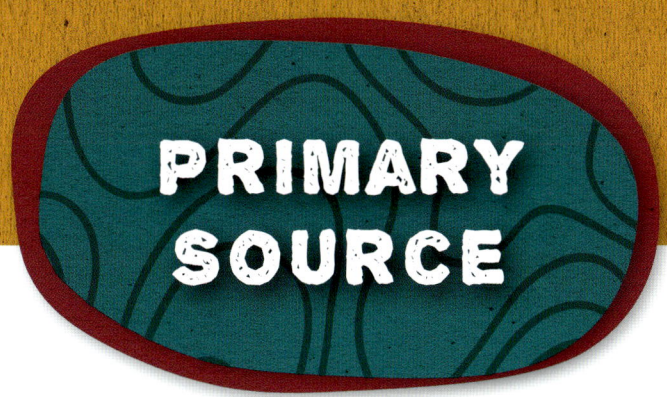

PRIMARY SOURCE

One Anangu said of the land around Uluru:

> We look after our place properly, looking after it together. . . . When we grow old and finish up the children that will follow will continue to have it.

Source: "Welcome from Anangu." *Australian Government Department of the Environment and Energy*, n.d., environment.gov.au. Accessed 16 Jan. 2020.

Comparing Texts

Think about the quote. Does it support the information in this chapter? Or does it give a different perspective? Explain in a few sentences.

An ocean once covered the area where Uluru now stands.

CHAPTER 2

FROM SEA TO DESERT

Uluru began forming 550 million years ago. At the time, the area was underwater. Ancient sea levels were higher than they are today. There were mountains nearby. **Sediment** from the mountains **eroded**. It settled where Uluru stands today.

Uluru used to be underground.

As mud and sand piled up, the sediment turned to rock.

Earth's land began to shift 400 million years ago. It pushed Uluru upward. Then 300 million years ago, sea levels dropped. Uluru rose up out of the ground. Wind and rain hit the rock. The wind and water eroded Uluru's surface. They shaped the rock. Uluru is always changing. So is the landscape around it.

Drying Out

About 65 million years ago, layers of mud and marine life surrounded Uluru. The climate became drier. Then, 500,000 years ago, the area became a desert. A thin layer of sand covered the dried mud from the seas.

Red Color

Uluru is made of a gray sandstone rock called arkose. Aboveground, minerals in the rock mixed with the air. The air made the minerals turn red.

Much of the rock Uluru is made of lies underground.

Uluru looks like a giant rock sitting on the ground. But scientists say most of Uluru is underground. Researchers believe the rest of Uluru lies up to 3.7 miles (6 km) deep under the ground.

Explore Online

Look at the website below. Does it give any new evidence to support Chapter Two?

Parks Australia: Amazing Facts

abdocorelibrary.com/uluru

Rainwater pours down Uluru's sides as waterfalls.

CAVES AND WATERFALLS

From far away, Uluru looks like it has smooth sides and a flat top. But up close, the effects of erosion are clear. There are cracks, caves, cliffs, and waterfalls.

The Mutitjulu Waterhole is on the eastern side of Uluru. It is one of the few places on Uluru that always has water. Water trickles over the ledges. An underground **spring** feeds the water hole. Trees line the edges of the hole. Birds sing in the branches.

Caves dot the steep sides of Uluru. One of these caves is Warayuki. Warayuki is sacred for Anangu men. Only Anangu men can visit it by

Red Centre

Red Centre is a part of central Australia. It has many beautiful landforms, including Uluru. Kings Canyon and Redbank **Gorge** are also in this area.

Mutitjulu Waterhole is a source of water for local wildlife.

Anangu law. Visitors to Uluru are not allowed at the cave. Other sites are sacred for Anangu women. These include Pulari on the southwest side of Uluru.

Tourists learn about Anangu rock art at the cave Kulpi Mutitjulu.

Anangu History

Paintings line many of Uluru's caves and formations. The paintings tell Anangu stories. They also teach Anangu laws. Anangu people say they have been on the land since creation.

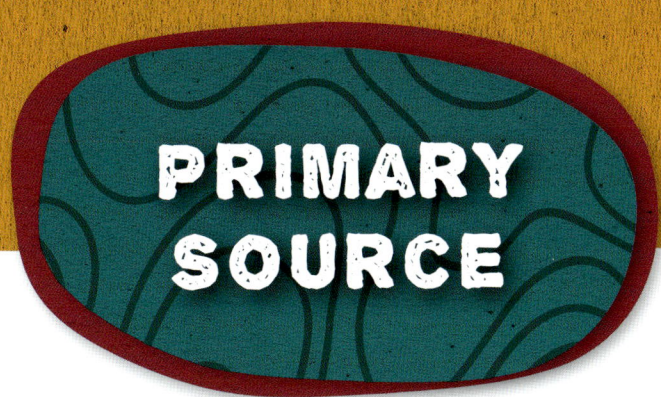

PRIMARY SOURCE

Marita Bradshaw is a geologist. She explains how erosion shapes Uluru.

> [Uluru] has been etched and polished over tens of millions of years to be the beautiful Uluru that we see now.

Source: Kylie Andrews. "How Uluru Formed over Millions of Years." *New Daily*, 27 June 2017, thenewdaily.com. Accessed 16 Jan. 2020.

Point of View

What is the author's point of view on what makes Uluru beautiful? What is your point of view? Write a short essay about how they are similar and different.

Kulpi Watiku is one of many caves around Uluru.

CHAPTER **4**

IN THE FUTURE

Uluru is always changing. Wind and rain carve gorges and cliffs. Tourism also has a big effect on the land. Anangu and the Australian government are both part of the Uluru-Kata Tjuta National Park board. This board protects Uluru.

Protecting Uluru

Uluru is part of a national park. The park protects the land and the plants and animals that live there. More than 250,000 people visit Uluru each year. Erosion speeds up when many people walk in the same place over and over. When people climbed Uluru, they left trash behind. This was bad for the environment. It was also disrespectful.

Animals

More than 200 **species** of animals call Uluru home. Visitors can spot eagles, pythons, kangaroos, and dingoes.

It is important that visitors stay on trails to protect the surrounding area.

Visiting the cultural center at Uluru is a great way to learn about the people who take care of Uluru.

Anangu live on the land around Uluru. They have their own laws. Anangu want people to visit Uluru. But they want visitors to respect the land. Anangu use Uluru to teach others about the land and about their culture. All people need to work together to protect this important and beautiful landform.

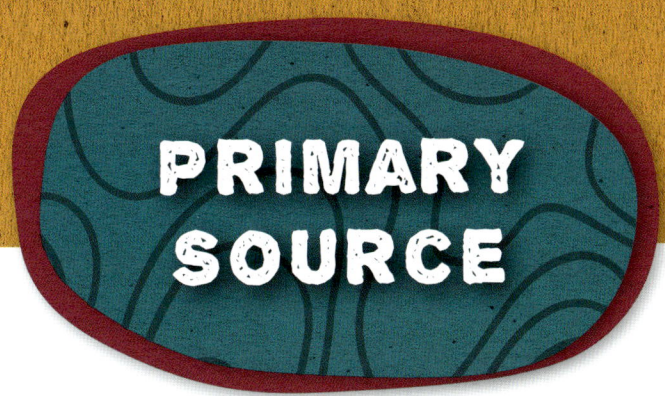

In 2017, the Uluru-Kata Tjuta National Park board announced visitors would not be allowed to climb Uluru after October 2019:

> The land has law and culture. We welcome tourists here. Closing the climb is not something to feel upset about but a cause for celebration.

Source: James Norman. "Why We Are Banning Tourists from Climbing Uluru." *Conversation*, 5 Nov. 2017, theconversation.com. Accessed 16 Jan. 2020.

What's the Big Idea?

Read this quote carefully. What is its main idea? Explain how the main idea is supported by details, naming one of those supporting details.

- Uluru began forming 550 million years ago.
- Uluru is 1,142 feet (348 m) tall.
- Each year, 250,000 people visit Uluru.

Glossary

eroded
became worn away by wind, water, and weather

gorge
a deep valley between two cliffs

sacred
important for religious reasons

sandstone
a type of rock made of sand-like quartz that has been pressed together with a cement-like material

sediment
sand, clay, and other loose material that can be moved by water or wind

species
different types of animals that look similar and are able to breed with other animals of the same type

spring
an underground source of water

Online Resources

To learn more about Uluru, visit our free resource websites below.

Visit **abdocorelibrary.com** or scan this QR code for free Common Core resources for teachers and students, including vetted activities, multimedia, and booklinks, for deeper subject comprehension.

Visit **abdobooklinks.com** or scan this QR code for free additional online weblinks for further learning. These links are routinely monitored and updated to provide the most current information available.

Learn More

Gaertner, Meg. *Rocks*. Abdo Publishing, 2020.

Gagne, Tammy. *Desert Ecosystems*. Abdo Publishing, 2016.

Sharif-Draper, Maryam. *Earth*. DK, 2017.

Index

age, 6, 11–13, 21
Anangu, 6, 8, 9, 18–20, 23, 26
animals, 24
Australia, 8, 18, 23

Bradshaw, Marita, 21

caves, 6, 17–20
climbing, 6, 24, 27

Eiffel Tower, 7
erosion, 11, 13, 17, 21, 24

Mutitjulu Waterhole, 18

paintings, 20
Pulari, 19

Red Centre, 18

sandstone, 6, 13
size, 6, 7, 15

tourism, 5, 19, 23–24, 26, 27

Uluru-Kata Tjuta National Park board, 23, 27

waterfalls, 6, 17

About the Author

Martha London writes books for young readers full-time. When she isn't writing, you can find her hiking in the woods.